D1709299

© 2022 Corianne Froese
Photos taken by Corianne Froese
All rights reserved.

No part of this book may be reproduced in any form whatsoever, whether by graphic, visual,
electronic, film, microfilm, tape recording, or any other means, without prior written permission of
the publisher, except in the case of brief passages embodied in critical reviews and articles.

The opinions and views expressed herein belong solely to the author and do not necessarily
represent the opinions or views of Cedar Fort, Inc. Permission for the use of sources, graphics, and
photos is also solely the responsibility of the author.

ISBN 13: 978-1-4621-4353-5

Published by Front Table Books, an imprint of Cedar Fort, Inc.
2373 W. 700 S., Springville, UT 84663
Distributed by Cedar Fort, Inc., www.cedarfort.com

Library of Congress Control Number: 2022941362

Cover design and interior layout and design by Courtney Proby
Cover design © 2022 Cedar Fort, Inc.
Typeset by Courtney Proby

Printed in the United States of America

10 9 8 7 6 5 4 3 2 1

Printed on acid-free paper

Cookie Couture

A GUIDE TO COOKIES
ALMOST TOO PRETTY TO EAT

CORIANNE FROESE

FRONT TABLE BOOKS • AN IMPRINT OF CEDAR FORT, INC. • SPRINGVILLE, UTAH

To Jeff—

You've cheered me on through every step of this journey while listening, encouraging, and going along with all my crazy ideas—even when they included pink glitter walls. Thank you for always keeping me caffeinated, laughing, and most of all, showing me what true unconditional love is.

To Parker and Kade—

I couldn't ask for better helpers, taste testers, and hype guys. You've been by my side since day one, and I hope you've seen that anything really is possible if you go for it and put in the work. Some of my most special memories are baking and decorating with you. You are my greatest accomplishments. I love you more than you'll ever know.

Contents

Seasonal Occasions

Tutorials

Resources

About the Author

Special Techniques to Highlight

My Story

You've seen them on the dessert tables, social media, and maybe have even been gifted some yourself—these little works of art that look far too pretty to eat . . . *almost.*

The true art of decorated sugar cookies has been around a long time, but only in recent years has it become a staple in the baking world. Go to any party or event, and chances are you'll see hand decorated, fully customized cookies to match. Some people look at them and wonder why on earth anyone would put that much effort into a cookie that's just going to be eaten. But for others, it sparks an interest that is sometimes enough to give it a try themselves. But where do you start?

My first set of royal icing cookies came about as a class treat for my oldest son, who was in preschool at the time and deep into the dinosaur phase. His birthday was approaching, and I told him we could send a treat for him to celebrate with his classmates—totally assuming I could just grab something store bought and call it a win. Without missing a beat, he was adamant that he needed to have dinosaur cookies to mark the occasion and that nothing else would do. I quickly regretted the decision to let him choose but decided I would see what I could do. Naturally I went online and was inundated with all kinds of recipes and blogs to sift through as I tried to find a straightforward path to success. I wasn't a baker and had never had any interest in it, but how hard could it really be? Little did I know what I was truly getting into, but I was officially invested and was determined to make my son's dinosaur dreams come true.

I may cringe when I look back on those first cookies now, but I was so proud at the time. My son was even prouder to share them with his class. Most people would breathe a sigh of relief and move on, but I wasn't finished just yet. Although I had a lot to learn about royal icing, consistencies, and all the little tricks and techniques for working with it, it was an eye-opening experience, and I made it my mission to perfect it.

Anyone who knew me at the time was an automatic beneficiary of my testing. Birthdays, baby showers, any reason to say thank you—there was a set of cookies for all of it! It was through my hands-on trials and errors that I soon started seeing the results I wanted, and suddenly people were asking me to make them for their occasions.

I had been a stay-at-home mom for five years, and this new hobby was so much more than just cookies. It was time I took for me to do something I personally loved, where the stresses and worries of life would fade and I was taken to a land of icing and sprinkles. This magical land presented me with a bucket list of new techniques I couldn't wait to try. Were there a lot of failures along the way? Absolutely, but that's the great thing about cookies—being able to eat the mess-ups and move on. Not once did my family think something wasn't good enough to eat. They always eagerly awaited my "reject cookies," as we called them.

The idea of turning this newfound passion into a small home business was daunting at first, but with the encouragement of family and friends, I decided I would give it a try. I mean, the demand was there, and I thought I might as well actually make some extra money if I was going to do it anyway!

Because there were no other cookie decorators in the area at the time, my little business went from 0–60 in what felt like overnight. Being able to make cookies for people's special occasions was something I enjoyed, not only for the decorating but also for hearing the stories behind each set. Custom cookies are so personal, and it was always a pleasure to bring their meaning to life.

As my business grew, I was not only doing custom orders but also offering predesigned holiday sets and participating in local markets. I even won an award for Small Business of the Year in our city. I also started teaching classes at a local art studio and sharing my tips and tricks on social media for beginners. The idea that cookies could have such an impact on others as it did for me has always been my motivator. I love seeing people find their own love for this art and am honored when I've had a part in helping them do so.

Along with others showing interest in my work, they also had questions about the tools and supplies I was using, which led to the next phase of my journey—opening a supply shop to offer all my favorite products, including some of my own. Although my days of selling cookies have passed, I love being able to create content and videos now to showcase our products and inspire others. It's truly amazing how something as simple as a cookie can change your life, whether you are just doing it as a hobby or have dreams of even more.

This book is, in a way, my journey coming full circle in getting to combine years of practice, trial and error, and beautiful successes into one place that can be a forever resource for all cookie enthusiasts to come. I'm so glad you're here and ready to get started!

And what do you actually need to get started? . . . Read on to find out!

Getting Started

TOOLS AND SUPPLIES

The first question I get from every new decorator is, "What do I *really* need to start?" The market is saturated with every bell and whistle, and while there are many things you'll want as you grow your skill set, there are some core tools and supplies that are essential for a successful start.

BAKING

MIXER: A handheld electric mixer is adequate to start, but you'll need to adjust some of the final steps and knead by hand as the motor won't be strong enough to complete it for you. A stand mixer is the most effective way to mix your dough and icing with ease.

MEASURING SPOONS & CUPS: It's always important to use accurate measurements when baking and to ensure that your tools are clean and free of any grease or residue.

FLEXIBLE SILICONE SPATULA: This is helpful for scraping and reincorporating ingredients from the sides and bottom of the mixing bowl where the paddle doesn't reach.

ROLLING PIN: Any basic rolling pin is adequate to start, but it is beneficial with sugar cookies to have one with built in or adjustable guides which ensures an even and consistent thickness for all of your cookies. A good width for sugar cookies is approximately $1/4$" - $5/16$".

SILICONE WORK MAT OR PARCHMENT PAPER: Roll your dough on either of these nonstick surfaces to reduce or eliminate the use of flour that can dry out your dough.

COOKIE CUTTERS AND CRAFT KNIFE: It's hard to know how many cookie cutters are truly ever enough! For the ones you don't have or for the shapes you can't find, you can use a paper cutout of the shape over the top of the dough and carefully hand cut it with a craft knife.

LARGE FLAT ANGLED SPATULA: This is helpful for transferring your cut-out shapes from the rolling surface to the cookie sheet and then to the cooling rack.

COOKIE SHEETS: Light colored aluminum-rimmed sheets are best for baking cookies. The most ideal sizes are ½ sheet (11.5 x 16.5 inches) and $3/4$ sheet (13 x 18 inches).

SILICONE BAKING LINERS: Silicone baking liners promote even heat distribution so that your cookies bake all the way through without prematurely browning on the bottoms. They also reduce the amount of spread. They must be kept free of grease buildup and wiped down after each baking session.

COOLING RACKS: Transfer your baked cookies from the cookie sheet to a cooling rack after a few minutes to fully cool them before decorating or storing them.

AIRTIGHT CONTAINERS: Keep your cookies fresh by storing them in airtight containers until you're ready to decorate them.

DECORATING

MIXING BOWLS: The number of bowls you need depends on how many colors you want to create; or you can rinse the same bowl in between colors. Ensure that the bowls you use are freshly cleaned and are kept exclusively for this purpose since any grease or residue in them can affect the integrity of the icing.

SILICONE SPATULAS: These are most ideal for creating consistencies and coloring your icing since you can scrape the bowl as you mix. They are also easy to rinse.

SPRAY BOTTLE: A little water goes a long way when creating different icing consistencies. Spraying in the water allows you to add small and controlled amounts.

DISPOSABLE TIPLESS PIPING BAGS AND CLIPS: A good piping bag is strong enough to resist bursting, yet comfortable to use so you can decorate with ease. Secure the top with a bag clip that you can adjust as you work. A tip clip can be used to close off the tip of the bag when not in use. The most ideal bag sizes for using with royal icing are 10 and 12 inches, and they can be rinsed and reused if you like.

PIPING TIPS: While you do not need a piping tip for piping borders and flooding, you will want them if you plan to do florals, ribbons, or ruffles. The most common ones are the petal, star, and v-shape.

SHARP SCISSORS: Cut the tip of your piping bags to the desired size and shape and to insert a piping tip.

SCRIBE TOOL: This is the most essential tool for working with royal icing to smooth it out, clean up the borders, and pop air bubbles. A simple needle or toothpick will work as well.

SMALL TABLETOP FAN: A cool air flow over your cookies in between steps results in more shine and a reduced chance of colors bleeding together, along with helping them crust over quicker so you can move on to your next steps sooner.

PAINT BRUSHES AND PALETTE: Having a variety of food safe brushes in different shapes like flat, angled, and fine tipped are useful for several decorating techniques. A palette with a lid will hold your ready-to-use paint or dust mixtures and allow you to store them for later use and reduced waste.

MINI TURNTABLE: Easily swivel your cookie as you work without the need to rotate with your hands. Especially useful for piping large florals.

FLOWER NAIL: With a flat circular top, you can pipe small floral icing transfers while rotating the nail with your thumb and forefinger.

ICING SCRAPER: The flat edge allows you to scrape icing evenly over the top of stencils and can be handy in creating straight lines with edible markers.

SILICONE ACCENT MOLDS: Some details are harder to pipe and can be better achieved by using a mold. Use chocolate or fondant to add these intricate accents to your cookies.

FOOD COLORS & DECORATIONS

Welcome to a world of possibilities! Color palettes and decorative elements are what bring a design to life and truly make them one of a kind.

FOOD COLORING: Both gels and dusts are best for tinting your icing. I always recommend that beginners start off with a good quality gel since gels are the most user friendly and easy to work with. Build your color by adding small amounts at a time and mixing to your desired shade. Keep in mind that colors will deepen as they have time to develop, so be sure not to oversaturate and give darker shades like black and red time to reach their full depth. It helps if you mix these the day prior to when you plan to decorate. Over-saturating your icing colors can also lead to the colors bleeding together.

A dust food coloring is dry pigment with no added preservatives. By using small amounts, you can achieve a much more intense color sooner. Because of how little dust is needed, you greatly reduce the risk of color bleed and avoid a bitter taste that can result from using too much gel. Most dust food colorings require a bit of water to activate them and seamlessly blend them into your icing. Applying them straight into your icing without fully dissolving them in water first can cause blotchiness or streaking.

TIPS FOR AVOIDING COLOR BLEED

1. Always add white pigment to your plain white icing to block other colors from bleeding into it. Use as little pigment as possible to achieve your desired shades. Some colors do need more pigment, so be aware of this and only add what is needed. You must also give darker colors time to develop.

2. Keep your flood icing at the 8–12 seconds consistency since runnier icing can bleed easier.

3. When flooding different colored sections next to each other, let one crust over before flooding the next. Wet to wet icing has a much higher chance of bleeding together. .

4. Use a table fan to crust the icing over quicker.

5. Never cover your cookies before they are fully dry.

EDIBLE MARKERS: Made with a food coloring-based ink, edible markers can be used to draw piping lines directly onto the bare cookie or icing to act as a guide. Enhance your overall designs by adding small details, text, and drawings to your fully dry icing. Ensure both the icing and marker areas are fully dry prior to packaging the cookies since any moisture can cause smudging. As a precaution, you can lightly dust the marker areas with cornstarch, which will absorb any potential moisture. .

SPRINKLES: Tie in your theme by accenting portions of your designs with matching sprinkles. You can strategically place certain shapes to act as elements, like buttons on a shirt or snowflakes on a tree. On cookies it's important to avoid any metallic, decorative-only pieces, because they cannot be removed prior to eating like they can be on a cake or another pastry

EDIBLE GLITTER: Add sparkle to your designs using food-safe glitter. Apply to icing that has just crusted and is still tacky so that it sits on top and retains its shimmer.

LUSTER AND PETAL DUSTS: These topical pigments can be dry dusted onto your icing to add shading, or they can be diluted with alcohol or an extract for painting and splattering. Luster dusts give a shimmer finish, and petal dusts give a matte finish. Use gold and silver luster dusts to paint metallic details.

It's always important to check the descriptions and labels for glitters and dusts to ensure they are food safe. Some, like a highlighter dust, are marked as "nontoxic" and are only intended for ornamental pieces that are to be removed prior to eating (for example, a sugar flower or a bow on a cake). It's always best to select fully edible options when using them on cookies.

Corianne's Sugar Cookie Recipe

Before you can get to the decorating, you need to bake your canvas. This recipe can do it all, whether you want to keep it classic or add in some fun with the variations. Best of all, it does not require chilling and will hold its shape well with a nice flat surface for decorating. The cookies are sturdy for working with while soft to the bite!

INGREDIENTS:

1½ cups (340.5 g) unsalted butter

2 cups (400 g) white granulated sugar

1 tsp salt

4 large eggs, cold

1 tbsp (15 ml) vanilla extract

1 tbsp (15 ml) vanilla bean paste (optional)

6 cups (752 g) all purpose flour

DIRECTIONS:

1. In the bowl of your stand mixer or with an electric mixer, cream together the room temperature butter, sugar and salt until smooth.

2. Add in the eggs, extract and paste, mixing until fully combined, use your spatula to scrape down the sides of the bowl when needed.

3. Add in all the flour at once and mix on a low speed until the dough pulls from the side of the mixing bowl.

Preheat oven to 390 degrees F. Roll the dough straight from the mixer on a non-stick baking mat or parchment paper, lightly dust the surface with flour if the dough sticks. There is no need to chill, as the cold eggs cool your dough. Roll the dough as few times as possible and incorporate new dough when you re-roll; overworking the same dough will lead to lumps and warping when baked.

Cut out your shapes and use an angled spatula to slide under and lift from the surface if needed. Place shapes onto a lined baking sheet about 1" apart and bake for 10–12 minutes, letting cool completely before storing or decorating.

If the dough is too sticky or dry, adjust the amount of flour until you reach a play dough-like texture. Every environment is different, and humidity can play a big role in how much flour you'll need.

Vanilla bean paste is optional but gives more flavor and can help with longer moisture. Play around with flavors too—almond and lemon are great alternatives to classic vanilla. Switch it up for the seasons with flavors like pumpkin spice or cinnamon too!

VARIATIONS

You can easily convert this to a chocolate base by substituting 1 cup of flour for 1 cup (100 g) of cocoa powder. Add the cocoa powder right after the eggs and flavoring. Combine and then proceed with the flour. The dough will be stickier but still manageable with a lightly floured rolling surface.

Mix in other elements at the same time as the flour, like chocolate chips or soft sprinkles to make a funfetti version. Use up to a cup of any dry ingredient you think would enhance the flavor or texture.

Gluten free? No problem. Simply switch out the all-purpose flour for a gluten-free 'cup for cup' blend.

SHELF LIFE, STORAGE & FREEZING

If you would like to prep the dough ahead of time, wrap it in plastic wrap and refrigerate for up to 1 week, or freeze up to 3 months. When ready to bake, let it come back to a just chilled temperature so that it is easy to work with but still cool.

Once your cookies are baked and completely cool to the touch, store them in an airtight container until you are ready to decorate. Ideally you want to start decorating within 1–2 days.

You can freeze baked sugar cookies for up to 3 months by placing them in a large Ziploc bag within an airtight container. Allow them to defrost completely in the container prior to opening again (overnight is the easiest). Opening prematurely will result in condensation that can cause them to form soggy patches or stick together.

Once you begin decorating, it's best to have them completed within 1–2 days when possible. Sugar cookies don't dry out quickly, but you do want to work efficiently to retain the moisture. Most designs take 8–12 hours between steps and dry times for the icing. Upon completion, you can store again in an airtight container for approximately 1 week.

Heat sealing cookies helps to preserve them much longer. (See page 131 for more on packaging.)

You can freeze fully decorated sugar cookies for 4–6 months. Either heat seal or place in a Ziploc bag and then into an airtight container. Again, the key is always how you defrost them. You must let them defrost completely in the container prior to opening. Opening prematurely will result in condensation that can cause your icing to become sticky and bleed together.

Corianne's Royal Icing Recipe

Royal icing is one of the most versatile for decorating and can take practice and patience to master. Every decorator will develop their own preference for how they like to work with it.

This recipe will give you a thick but flexible piping consistency to start with. You will then create your other consistencies by adding water for flooding or more icing sugar for thicker elements. The light corn syrup gives the icing a glossier finish and keeps it soft to the bite while still being able to stack and package normally.

INGREDIENTS:

1/2 cup (118 ml) warm water

1/2 tsp (2.5 ml) clear, oil free flavouring

5 tbsp (75 g) meringue powder

5 cups (605 g) icing sugar

2 tbsp (30 ml) light corn syrup

DIRECTIONS:

1. Whisk together water, meringue powder, and extract in your mixer bowl until frothy.

2. Gradually add icing sugar on low with your mixer's paddle attachment.

3. Once combined, add light corn syrup, and mix on a medium to high speed for 2 minutes. Do not overmix.

ICING CONSISTENCIES

Consistency can be the most challenging part of decorating to master but is the most important. It can take some trial and error, but you WILL find your way with it. If you find that any of your consistencies aren't ideal when decorating, take them back to the mixing bowl and adjust them. This can mean adding more icing sugar to thicken it, or water to thin it. It takes more time but will make a world of difference for learning what works best, and you'll see the results that you want sooner.

I always prefer to use two consistencies – piping for the borders and flood for filling the inside. Some decorators choose to use a medium consistency between the two that can achieve both, but you do have to work the icing more with a scribe to settle it. I like to let the flood icing do the work and settle on its own, which also saves time when doing large batches.

Piping consistency is thick but flexible and will hold its form, like toothpaste. I take icing straight from the mixer for this and use it for piping borders and most details. You should be able to hold your mixer paddle upright and see the icing curl. Adjust the batch with a little water or icing sugar if needed to achieve this result.

Color then icing at this stage so that it's the same shade when creating other consistencies from it. Learn more about Food coloring on page 6.

Add the amount you would like for the piping consistency to a piping bag and move on to creating the flood consistency.

Flood consistency is like honey where it has a slow flow and some body to it. It's used to fill the center of the cookie and settles completely flat. For this you will add very small amounts of water at a time, mixing it just to the point where it will glide / ribbon off the spatula.

A good method for getting the right flood is to cut a line down the middle of the icing with the spatula and count how long it takes to settle back into the bowl completely level (as you would want it to on the actual cookie to give a nice and smooth surface). An effective flood icing will take between 8 and 12 seconds to settle. If it's not settling, continue to mix small amounts of water at a time until it does. If it's settling too soon, mix in small amounts of icing sugar to thicken it back up to where it should be.

Mixing the water into your icing also naturally incorporates air which leads to unwanted bubbles when decorating. Let your flood icing rest, covering the bowl with a damp cloth to allow the bubbles to rise to the top of the icing. Wait about 10 minutes and then run your spatula over them to pop prior to bagging.

Since freshly made icing has more air in it, it can help to add existing icing into a new batch to make it denser and less prone to bubbles. You can also get some great shades this way if the existing icing is already colored! If you have several unused colors left over, mix them all up to make black.

Thick consistency icing is mostly used for florals, stenciling and more intricate borders as it maintains its form completely when piped. Add small amounts of icing sugar at a time to your piping consistency until it holds a stiff peak on the spatula. You want it thick enough to hold its form, but not so thick that it's hard to pipe.

Royal icing dries out extremely fast when exposed to air, so it's important to cover your bowl with a damp towel between preparation steps.

Royal icing doesn't necessarily go bad but instead loses its volume over time, making it less desirable to work with—you'll know just by looking at it when it's time to discard it.

Ensure your containers are airtight when storing for longer periods of time. You can store on the counter if using within a day, in the fridge for up to 2 weeks, or in the freezer for 2–3 months. When freezing, let the container come back to room temperature before using because it's hard to gauge the true consistency of cold icing. Combine in the mixer again prior to using.

You should aim to bag your icing when you are ready to use it and refrigerate flood consistencies during any time gaps. Refrigerating helps prevent separation of flood consistencies, which have more water content—you may notice slight separation even when leaving a flood bag on the counter for a few hours. Always massage bags if they've been sitting for a bit to prevent your icing from becoming streaky, and refrigerate if not working with it for an extended period.

When possible, incorporate your existing icing into fresh batches. Older icing is denser and will weigh down your new airy icing, making for less bubbles. And, it is a bit easier to work with.

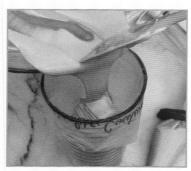
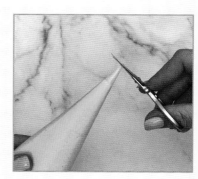

FILLING & CUTTING A PIPING BAG

Disposable piping bags are the preferred method for cookie decorating, not just for convenience but also comfort. They come with a completely closed tip that you can cut to fit a stainless-steel tip, or you can go tipless and cut the ends to your desired width.

Use a narrow cup to hold the piping bag as you fill it and tie or secure with a clip. A ¾ full, 12" piping bag holds enough icing to cover 12–18 standard sized cookies.

For piping without a tip, flatten the tip of the bag with the seam to the side and cut straight across. You just need a few mm off the tip for your thicker piping consistency and slightly more for the flood bag. Smooth the tip back to a circular opening. If the thicker icing curls when coming out, cut the hole slightly wider. Remember, you can always cut off more, but you can't add it back! Use a tip clip to close off the tip between use

  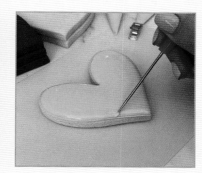

THE BASICS OF PIPING & FLOODING

1. Use your piping consistency to create a border around the edge of your cookie. Touch down the icing at your starting point while lifting and applying an even pressure, letting the icing fall along the edge. Dragging the tip of the bag along the cookie will result in a jagged edge. Let the border crust over for about a minute before flooding.

2. Apply the flood icing evenly and so that it sits just above the border without spilling over. The border can be visible but shouldn't protrude above the flood to give a nice and clean look. You can start around the edge and work in, or vice versa depending on your comfort level. A good flood icing will settle mostly on its own. Let it do the work for you. If your icing ends up running off the cookie, it's likely too thin. If it isn't settling nicely even when manipulated with a scribe, it's too thick.

3. Use a scribe tool, toothpick, or needle to clean up the edges and pop any air bubbles that arise before the flood icing starts to crust over. Always drag the air bubble to the side to pop it and don't poke it inward, as it will re-emerge later when it's too late to fix it.

If adding sprinkles, do so while the icing is wet so they are held in when it dries.

Once the flood has set, the cookie should never be lifted but slid across the work surface until it's mostly dry. Lifting or moving it around too much will cause cracks to form across the surface.

Position the freshly iced cookie in front of a small table fan for about 10 minutes. This helps the icing crust over faster and adds more shine.

TIMING YOUR DETAILS

Most details are done with the piping and thicker consistencies. Simple icing details and writing can be applied 1–2 hours after the flood icing has crusted over; you still want to be careful though not to puncture the surface. You can also pipe florals or add other elements like fondant pieces around this time. Painting and airbrushing can typically be done after about 6 hours of dry time and stenciling with icing or writing with edible markers around the 10-hour mark. Refer to pages 123 and 127 for more of stencilling and airbrushing.

LETTERING

Like anything with decorating, consistency is key for writing with royal icing. I generally use my piping consistency, as you want it thick enough to hold its form with a bit of

softness to manipulate if needed—again, think toothpaste with that slight curl at the end!

It can really help to practice before taking your skills to the actual cookie. You can find some fonts online, print them, and place a piece of parchment over the top of to practice on. This will allow you to see if your consistency is correct and how to time the amount of pressure that you apply to the bag.

When using handwritten or calligraphy style fonts, the general rule is to go harder and slower for the downstroke and lighter and faster upward. Gradually lighten the pressure and release at the end, using a scribe immediately to smooth out any areas before they crust over.

An alternative to writing with icing is to do so with an edible marker. A dual tipped marker is great because you can use the thin and thicker ends to achieve different styles. Have a damp paintbrush on hand to fix any areas if needed, and remember that the cookie must be fully dry prior to writing on it.

If you plan to do a lot of writing, it can be worthwhile to invest in a mini projector and mount. These projectors connect to your computer or mobile device to display any image onto the cookie so that you can simply trace it with the perfect placement and spacing. This is especially useful for logos or character work. Most projectors will require an HDMI cable and adapter specific to the device you are displaying from. The exact requirements should be noted by the manufacturer.

DRY TIME

While different environments effect dry times, most decorated cookies need a full 10–12 hours of airtime to become completely dry. Icing acts like a sealant to lock in the moisture of the cookie, so you won't experience your cookie drying out in this time. If you find that your icing won't dry, it could be humidity related or a result of overmixing the icing beyond the 2 minutes recommended. It's also important to use oil-free flavorings in your icing. Flavorings with oil can cause greasy patches that do not dry.

Prematurely covering your cookies before the icing is fully dry will lead to color bleed because of the trapped moisture. Never cover them before 10–12 hours have passed.

Packaging your cookies can be as simple as an airtight container, or you can invest in an impulse heat sealer and clear cellophane bags so that they can be placed in a bakery box without drying out. Heat sealing cookies extends their shelf life to at least 2 weeks (often even longer) and gives you flexibility as to when you can make them for an event.

TROUBLESHOOTING

ICING THAT DOESN'T FULLY DRY

Never mix more than 2–3 minutes at high speed in the mixer, as it can lead to icing that doesn't fully dry, as well as more air bubbles, color bleed, and lack of body. Do not use flavorings that contain oil, and ensure that all your equipment is clean and free of any oil as well.

AIR BUBBLES

It's always best to try to reduce the amount of air bubbles in flood icing before using as it will save you time and frustration when decorating. They can be greatly reduced by simply letting your prepared flood icing sit covered in the mixing bowl for at least 10 minutes. This allows the bubbles to rise to the top so you can pop them with a spatula prior to using.

STREAKY ICING

If your colours are showing streaks, it can mean that you didn't mix your food color thoroughly, or that your icing has been sitting unused for too long in the bag. A quick re-stirring or massage of the bag should fix this.

CRATERING

Cratering in icing is the concaving of small or narrow flood areas that only appear once the icing has dried. They can be hard to fix and very discouraging, but you can avoid them with the right icing consistencies and my anti-cratering technique.

You'll notice that many of my designs use squiggles within certain flood areas—these act as a support to the thinner flood icing placed afterward. You want to keep your flood icings on the thicker side for these areas. In addition, you can immediately place the cookie in front of a table fan so that it can crust over right away and stay level.

Cratering can also happen when piping smaller details with too thin of a consistency where it then forms a hole over the surface once dry. Use piping consistency for detail work, smoothing with a scribe as needed so that it's thick and can hold its form. Placing in front of a fan afterward will also ensure that these unwanted holes don't form.

OILY LOOKING PATCHES

Blotchy icing can be the result of the butter from the cookie bleeding into the icing. Humid climates are more prone to this and can avoid it by letting the freshly baked and fully cooled cookie sit covered in a container for at least a day before decorating. It can also help to use a slightly thicker flood consistency, as a thinner icing will absorb butter bleed much easier. If you have already decorated and have these spots on your icing, try setting the cookies on a baking sheet and putting it in the oven with the door cracked open at a low temp for a few minutes to try and even it out. Often the butter bleed fades and isn't noticeable to an untrained eye.

Birthday

Sure, everyone gets a cake for their birthday, but not a set of cookies! While this set is made up of classic shapes, you can tie in favorite colors and add their name or a personalized message to the central plaque for that extra special touch.

This set works with all the consistency types and luster dust for various paint techniques. I always love the look of a black outline and how it gives a more modern look. The cotton candy sprinkle mix was the inspiration for my icing colors and of course, nothing is complete without some edible glitter!

COOKIE SHAPES:

- Balloon
- Present
- Candle
- Plaque
- Cupcake

DECORATING TOOLS:

- 9 piping bags
- Paint palette
- Clips
- Paint brushes (flat, fan & dot)
- Scribe tool

ICING COLORS & CONSISTENCIES:

- Piping and flood consistencies in pink and black
- Flood consistency in pink, purple, blue & yellow
- Thick consistency in purple

DECORATIONS & COLORANTS:

- Coordinating sprinkle mix
- Alcohol
- Edible glitter
- Orange edible marker
- Gold luster dust

Both luster (shimmer) and petal (matte) dusts can be used as a paint by diluting with a small amount of alcohol. An alcohol base is best as it evaporates when applied, leaving just the pigment whereas water sits over the icing longer and can eat away at the icing. There is no aftertaste once the alcohol has evaporated, and your icing is still safe for consumption. You can use vodka or an alcohol-based activator which has additional ingredients to enhance the way the paint glides and adheres.

Add some dust to your palette and mix in small amounts of alcohol at a time until you reach a consistency like acrylic paint. If it becomes too runny, add more dust to thicken it back. Only prepare your paint when you are ready to use it as with the evaporation rate of alcohol, it will dry up when left unused. You may need to mix in small amounts as you work to keep the consistency. A lidded palette is beneficial as you can cover the remaining dust to activate again later.

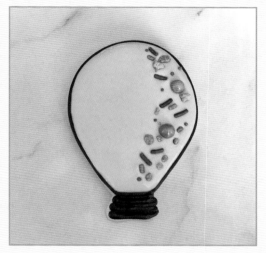

1. Outline with black piping icing, adding a ribbed effect to the bottom tie.

2. Fill with blue flood icing so that the black border is still visible.

3. Add sprinkles along one side while the flood icing is still wet.

4. Once the flood icing has crusted over, lightly splatter gold paint over top with a flat paint brush and apply edible glitter.

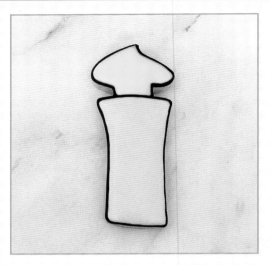

1. Outline the candle and flame with black piping icing.

2. Use flood icing to fill the candle with pink and the flame with yellow, ensuring the black borders remain visible.

3. Once the flood icing is fully dry, lightly brush gold paint over the top and bottom of the candle with a fan brush and apply edible glitter over top.

4. Draw a few lines on the flame with an orange edible marker and blend with a damp paint brush followed by edible glitter.

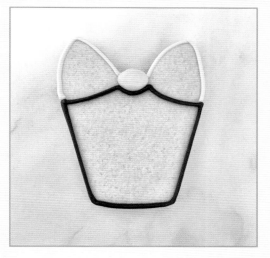

1. Use piping icing to outline the box with black and the bow with pink. Pipe a dot from the center outward in the middle of the bow, using a scribe tool to smooth out. Place the cookie in front of a fan for 5 minutes so that the dot does not crater.

2. Use flood icing to fill the box with purple and the bow with pink while ensuring the black border remains visible.

3. Once the flood icing has crusted over, apply edible glitter to the bow and use black piping icing to outline around the bow.

4. Once the flood icing is fully dry, apply dots with gold paint and a round dot brush.

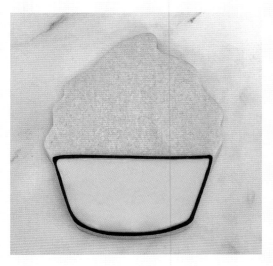

1. Outline the base of the cupcake with black piping icing.

2. Fill with blue flood icing so that the black border is still visible.

3. Once the flood icing has crusted over, lightly splatter gold paint over top with a flat paint brush and use the black piping icing to pipe vertical lines across.

4. Use a thick icing to pipe the top of the cupcake in purple. Add sprinkles and top with edible glitter.

1. Outline with black piping icing.

2. Fill with pink flood icing so that the black border is still visible.

3. Once the flood icing is fully dry, lightly brush gold paint over the top left and bottom right followed by edible glitter.

4. Use the black piping icing to write Happy Birthday or any other special message.

Wedding

The most important day of someone's life deserves all the personal touches. Custom cookies add such a special element to a dessert table and can also make a great take along favor for guests!

Florals are the star of any wedding cookie set and if you're looking for that extra wow, silicone molds will give you a level of detail that you just can't get with royal icing flowers. These molds work great with fondant and chocolate, but not royal icing as it doesn't dry fully inside of them. The great part is that you can make these accents in advance and even have a variety on hand to speed up future projects!

COOKIE SHAPES:

- Bow tie
- Floral cake on stand
- Floral wedding ring
- Square floral plaque
- Wedding dress

DECORATING TOOLS:

- 8 piping bags
- Clips
- V shaped leaf piping tip
- Scribe tool
- Icing scraper
- Paint palette
- Brushes (dust, stiff, angled & flat)
- Floral silicone mold

ICING COLORS & CONSISTENCIES:

- Piping and flood consistencies in white & black
- Piping consistency in brown, pink & dark green
- Thick consistency in light green

DECORATIONS & COLORANTS:

- Fondant
- Burgundy gel or petal dust color
- Cornstarch
- Edible glitter
- Pearl and gold luster dusts
- Alcohol
- Black & brown edible markers

(See page 26 for painting with dusts.)

I like to use ready made fondant for my accents which you can get pre colored or in white to tint yourself with any gel or petal dust food coloring. You can dry dust, paint and airbrush them too depending on the look you would like!

Fondant is like an edible play doh and can be hard in texture at first. If it doesn't soften enough to work with by kneading with your hands, place in the microwave for up to 5 seconds and it will become much softer. Once its ready, massage in the burgundy food coloring until it is fully saturated.

STEPS FOR MAKING FONDANT ACCENTS

1. Brush the cavity of the mold with a bit of cornstarch to help the fondant release nicely and not stick inside.

2. Press your fondant in and scrape away any excess from the back with the side of your scribe. You should be able to remove the fondant from the mold right away but if you find that you are having issues, just set it in the freezer for a few minutes.

3. Gently remove by bending the mold and letting it come out naturally.

Let your accents firm up for half an hour before further handling and use a bit of royal icing to glue onto the cookie once ready. They do hold their form well but you should still be careful not to put too much pressure on them if packaging. If making in advance, store in an airtight container away from direct sunlight for up to 3 months.

1. Outline the top portion of the cake with white piping icing and fill with white flood icing.

2. Once halfway dry, use a brown edible marker to lightly draw guides that define the cake.

3. Use an icing scraper to lightly spread brown piping icing across to cake portion.

4. Outline the cake stand with white piping icing, adding squiggles inside to prevent cratering and fill with white flood icing. Set in front of a fan for 5-10 minutes to prevent cratering.

5. Once fully dry, paint with gold and pipe the loops with black piping icing.

6. Pressure pipe the darker greenery with piping icing in a tear drop motion, applying hard and slow pressure at first and lighter as you pull away. Use a v shaped leaf tip to pipe the light green leaves with thick icing, applying more pressure at first and lighter as you release. Pipe the brown straight lines and pink dots at the end with piping icing.

Continued on pg. 36

7. Use a bit of icing to glue the fondant flowers in place.

Bow Tie

1. Outline with black piping icing.

2. Fill with black flood icing.

3. Once fully dry, dry brush pearl luster dust over the surface of the icing.

4. Outline again with black piping icing to give definition.

1. Use a circular item to trace an inside piping guide with an edible marker.

2. Outline with white piping icing, adding squiggles inside the band and diamond to prevent cratering.

3. Fill the band with white flood icing and set in front of a fan for 5-10 minutes to prevent cratering.

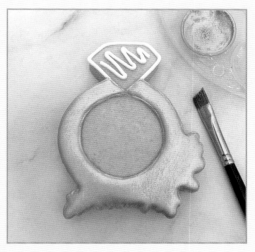

4. Once half way dry, lightly paint with gold.

Continued on pg. 38

5. Fill the diamond with flood icing and set in front of a fan for 5-10 minutes. Add some edible glitter to the diamond once it has crusted over and outline with white piping icing for definition.

6. Pressure pipe the darker greenery with piping icing in a tear drop motion, applying hard and slow pressure at first and lighter as you pull away. Use a v shaped leaf tip to pipe the light green leaves with thick icing, applying more pressure at first and lighter as you release. Pipe the brown straight lines and pink dots at the end with piping icing.

7. Use a bit of icing to glue the fondant flowers in place and add some definition to the band with a black edible marker.

1. Outline with white piping icing.
2. Fill with white flood icing.

3. Use the edge of an icing scraper or other food safe straight edged object to draw evenly spaced lines both vertically and horizontally with a black edible marker.

4. Use a black edible marker to write 'We Do' across the top—you could do also do the last name of the couple or 'save the date' if using for a wedding shower. Write the numeric date of the wedding in one of the squares with a red heart around it

5. Pressure pipe the darker greenery with piping icing in a tear drop motion, applying hard and slow pressure at first and lighter as you pull away. Use a v-shaped leaf tip to pipe the light green leaves with thick icing, applying more pressure at first and lighter as you release. Pipe the brown straight lines and pink dots at the end with piping icing.

Continued on pg. 40

6. Use a bit of icing to glue the fondant flower in place and add some definition around the edge of the cookie with a brown edible marker.

Dress

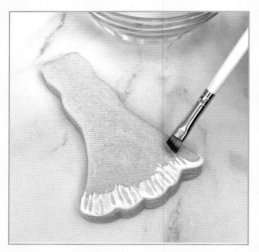

1. Pipe white flood icing along the bottom of the dress in small sections and brush inward with a stiff angled paint brush. Wipe off any excess icing as you go and dampen the brush with a little bit of water if needed to help it spread smoothly.

2. Add edible glitter and pipe the outline for the rest of the dress with white piping icing.

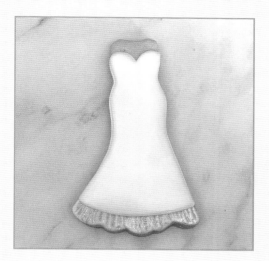

3. Fill the dress with white flood icing.

4. Once fully dry, dry brush pearl luster dust over the surface.

5. Pipe a belt with black piping icing and apply the fondant accent to it while it's still wet.

Gender Reveal

Because waiting is hard! There's nothing like being one of the first to know when creating these cookies that reveal the secret inside. Break in half or take a big bite to reveal the surprise!

Before baking, create a cavity in the middle of your cut out shape using a knife for the outline and a spoon to scoop it out. Be careful not to warp the overall shape of the cookie and ensure the bottom of the cavity doesn't have any holes or gaps that will let the icing show through the bottom. There's no need to adjust the time or temperature and you can bake as usual.

When using white as the base colour for the onesie, add a little extra white food coloring to the icing so that it blocks the colour inside from showing through. Use a light tone for the surprise colour inside as you don't want to chance any spoilers!

COOKIE SHAPE:

- Baby onesie

ICING COLORS & CONSISTENCIES:

- Piping and flood consistencies in white
- Piping consistency in black, pink and blue
- Flood consistency in pink or blue

DECORATIONS & COLORANTS:

- Gold luster dust
- Alcohol

DECORATING TOOLS:

- 6 piping bags
- Clips
- Scribe tool
- Paint palette
- Detail paint brush

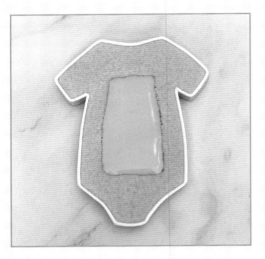

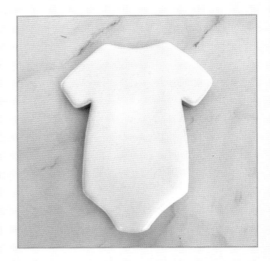

1. Fill the inside of the cavity with the flood icing color that represents the gender and let dry for at least 2 hours.

2. Outline the onesie with white piping icing.

3. Fill with white flood icing.

4. Once fully crusted over, use the black, pink and blue piping icings to write the 'He or She' and white piping icing for the question mark. You could also incorporate the last name of the couple, due date or anything else special.

5. Paint the question marks in gold (see page 26 for painting with dusts).

TIP: Use the same color of icing as the base to pipe the details that you plan to paint. If you miss any spots, it won't be as noticeable!

Baby Shower

A classic baby shower set never goes out of style and beautiful cookies can double as both a dessert and decor!

Now I know I could have gone neutral on this set but being a boy mom, I have to live a little. I especially wanted to showcase how even simple florals like these rosettes can still make a statement. I always suggest practicing your florals first before you pipe them directly onto the cookie to ensure that you have the right consistency and technique.

COOKIE SHAPES:

- Bib
- Bottle
- Dress
- Mobile
- Rattle

DECORATING TOOLS:

- 10 piping bags
- Clips
- 3 star shaped piping tips
- 1 V shaped leaf piping tip
- Scribe tool
- Paint palette
- Paint brushes (stiff angled & detail)
- Star silicone mold

ICING COLORS & CONSISTENCIES:

- Piping and flood consistencies in white, light pink & dark pink
- Flood consistency in green
- Thick consistency in light pink, medium pink, dark pink & green

DECORATIONS & COLORANTS:

- Fondant
- Pink gel or petal dust color
- Cornstarch
- Edible glitter
- Rose gold luster dust
- Alcohol
- Black edible marker

ROYAL ICING TRANSFERS

You can also make florals or any small royal icing decoration in advance as a transfer. Pipe the icing directly onto parchment and let fully dry before removing. Its best to use thick icing consistency for florals and piping icing for other shapes so that they hold their form. Templates can be used underneath the parchment as well to act as a guide for specific shapes. Use a bit of icing to position the transfers in place on the cookie - this method is great as you can experiment with placement or different sizes prior!

See page 26 for painting with dusts.
See page 34 for creating fondant accents.

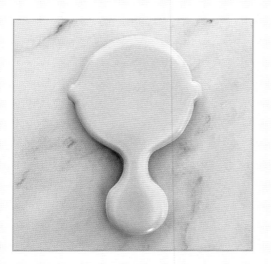

1. Outline with light pink piping icing.

2. Fill with light pink flood icing.

3. Once crusted over, use medium pink thick icing and star tip to pipe the rosette in a swirl motion, releasing lightly at the end and blend with a scribe tool if needed. Use a v shaped leaf tip to pipe the green leaf, applying more pressure at first and lighter as you release. Use piping icing to pipe the light and dark pink lines and loops.

4. Once fully dry, paint the light pink lines and dots in rose gold and add some lines and dots for definition with black edible marker (see page 26 for painting with dusts).

1. Use piping icing to outline to bottle portion with white, nozzle with dark pink and nipple with light pink. Add squiggle lines inside the nozzle and nipple to prevent cratering.

2. Fill the bottle with white flood icing and nipple with light pink.

3. Once crusted over, fill the nozzle with dark pink flood icing.

4. Once the nozzle has crusted over, pipe continuous loops with dark pink piping icing.

5. Use light, medium and dark pink thick icing with star tips to pipe the side by side rosettes in a swirl motion, releasing lightly at the end and blend with a scribe tool if needed. Use a v shaped leaf tip to pipe the green leaves, applying more pressure at first and lighter as you release. Use white piping icing to pipe the dots.

Continued on pg. 50

6. Once fully dry, paint the white dots with rose gold and draw on the measurements and definition lines with black edible marker.

Mobile

1. Outline the cloud with white piping icing.

2. Fill the cloud with white flood icing.

3. Pipe lines from the mobile down with white piping icing and place the fondant stars (or star sprinkles) so that the icing holds them.

4. Once the white flood icing has crusted over, use light pink piping icing to pipe the looped border along the top of the cloud and lightly paint the fondant accents with rose gold.

5. Once full dry, draw closed eyelids with lashes in the middle of the cloud with black edible marker.

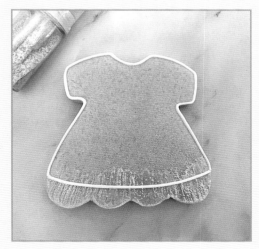

1. Pipe light pink flood icing along the bottom of the dress in sections at a time and brush inward with a stiff angled paint brush. Wipe off any excess icing as you go and dampen the brush with a little bit of water if needed to help it spread nicely.

2. Add edible glitter and pipe the outline for the rest of the dress with white piping consistency.

3. Use flood icings to fill the dress with white and immediately add dark pink dots. Use your scribe tool to swirl the dots around until they resemble a rose. Add a dot of green flood icing beside it and drag outward with the scribe to form a leaf shape. Work quickly so that the icing doesn't start to crust over before the design is complete.

Continued on pg. 52

4. Once crusted over, use light pink or white piping icing to pipe the ribbon belt, dots for the pearl necklace and tear drops for the bottom beading. For the beading, apply hard and slow pressure at first and lighter as you release.

5. Once fully dry, paint the belt, necklace and bottom beading with rose gold Brush a bit of paint down the light pink brushed bottom icing and add some lines and dots for definition with black edible marker.

Bib

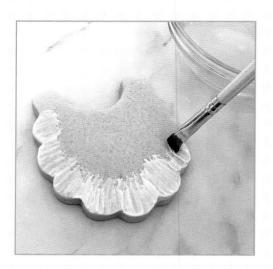

1. Pipe white flood icing along the bottom of the bib and brush inward with a stiff angled paint brush. Wipe off any excess icing as you go and dampen the brush with a little bit of water if needed to help it spread nicely.

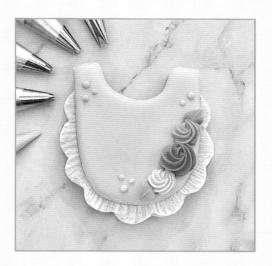 

2. Add some edible glitter and pipe the outline for the rest of the bib with light pink piping icing.

3. Fill the bib with light pink flood icing.

4. Once crusted over, use light, medium and dark pink thick icing with star tips to pipe the side by side rosettes in a swirl motion, releasing lightly at the end and blend with a scribe tool if needed. Use a v shaped leaf tip to pipe the green leaves, applying more pressure at first and lighter as you release. Use light pink piping icing to pipe the dots.

5. Once fully dry, paint the light pink dots in rose gold and add some lines and dots for definition with black edible marker.

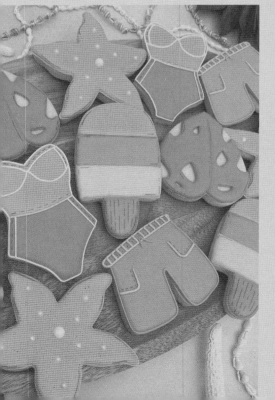

Valentine's Day

Show your loved ones how special they are with these extra sweet designs. These lip cookie pops always lead to some fun photos too – just add photography prop to the list of what cookies can do!

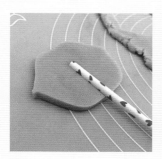 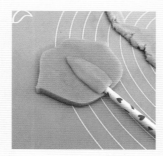 

HOW TO BAKE COOKIE POPS:

1. Cut out your dough shape and flip over on a non stick surface like a baking liner or parchment paper.

2. Gently push a paper straw into the dough about halfway, patching the back of the straw with some more dough.

3. Place the dough with the straw underneath on the baking sheet and add some scrap dough between them if needed to prevent hot spots and uneven baking.

Out of everything I bake, these little crispy scraps are my families favorite to snack on after! And don't worry - the straws won't burn, I promise.

COOKIE SHAPES:

- Chocolate kiss
- Ice cream cone
- Lip
- Mini heart
- Strawberry

DECORATING TOOLS:

- Piping bags
- Clips
- Scribe tool
- Print brushes (dust & fan)

ICING COLORS & CONSISTENCIES:

- Piping and flood consistencies in red, pink, blue, purple, yellow, green, light brown, dark brown and white

- Piping consistency in black

DECORATIONS & COLORANTS:

- Coordinating sprinkle mix

- Edible glitter

- Pearl luster dust

- Black edible marker

Lip Pops

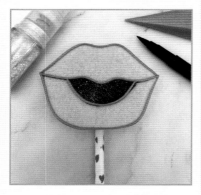  

1. Use a black edible marker to draw on the lip creases and the opening of the mouth. Apply edible glitter over the opening of the mouth right away.

2. Outline all areas with red piping icing and fill the bottom lip with red flood icing.

3. Once the bottom lip has crusted over, fill the top with red flood icing.

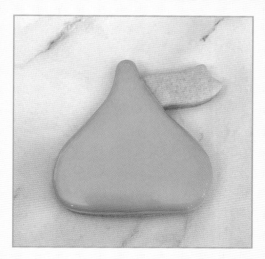

1. Outline the chocolate portion with blue piping icing

2. Fill with blue flood icing and let dry for at least 2 hours.

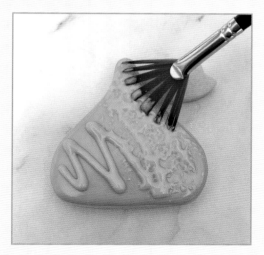

3. Add some flood icing to the top and blot with a fan brush to create texture.

4. Once the texture is dry, use a dust brush to apply a light and even layer of pearl luster dust.

5. Outline the tab with white piping icing and add squiggle lines inside to prevent cratering. Fill with white flood icing.

6. Once fully dry, write a message on the tab with black edible marker.

Ice Cream Cone

1. Use piping icing to outline the cone with light brown and three ice cream scoops with pink.

2. Fill the middle scoop with pink flood icing and apply sprinkles to the top half. Fill the cone with light brown flood icing.

3. Once the first two sections have crusted over, pipe crisscrossed lines over the cone with light brown piping icing and fill the bottom and top ice cream scoops with pink flood icing. Apply sprinkles to the top scoop and edible glitter once crusted over.

Conversation Heart

1. Outline the hearts with purple and yellow piping icing.

2. Fill the hearts with purple and yellow flood icing.

3. Once fully dry, write a message or saying with black edible marker.

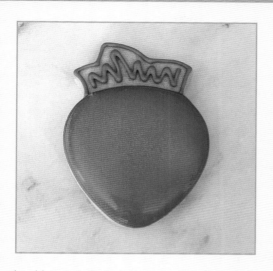

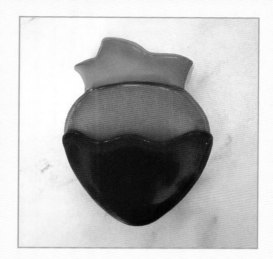

1. Use piping icing to outline the strawberry in red and leaves in green with squiggle lines to prevent cratering.

2. Fill the strawberry with red flood icing and let crust over.

3. Fill the leaves with green flood icing.

4. Outline the dipped chocolate with dark brown piping icing.

5. Fill the dipped chocolate with dark brown flood icing and let crust over.

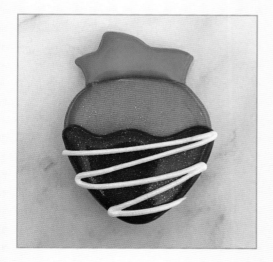

6. Pipe the drizzled chocolate with white piping icing and add some edible glitter.

St. Patrick's Day

Even simple cookies can still make a statement! If you are looking to save some time while still getting that wow effect, marbled cookies are for you. Take a simple shape that represents the occasion and use a color combination that will combine nicely when blended.

The key to dipping is using a flood consistency that will settle on its own while not running off the sides of the cookie – I find this to be right in the 7-10 second range. To time your icing, cut a line down the middle of it with a spatula and count how long it takes to settle back into the bowl completely level. Add small amounts of water to thin it down or icing sugar to thicken.

It's very important when dipping to eliminate as many air bubbles as possible prior. Let your flood icing rest, covering the bowl with a damp cloth to allow the bubbles to rise to the top of the icing. Wait about 10 minutes and then run your spatula over to pop them before starting.

COOKIE SHAPES:

- Shamrock or 4 leaf clover

DECORATING TOOLS:

- 1 piping bag
- Clips
- Scribe tool
- Small bowl

ICING COLORS & CONSISTENCIES:

- Flood consistency in light and dark green

DECORATIONS & COLORANTS:

- Coordinating sprinkle mix

1. Using 7-10 second flood consistencies, pipe dark green over a base light green in a bowl and swirl it around with a scribe tool.

2. Dip the front of the cookie so that there is even coverage and pull upward, letting the excess icing run back into the bowl. You can shake the cookie or use the side of the bowl to help get as much off as possible.

3. Flip the cookie over and smooth out if needed with a scribe tool, gently popping any visible air bubbles.

4. Add coordinating sprinkles to one side.

5. Repeat the process, adding more dark green icing to the top and swirling it as you go

Spring: Cookie Bouquet

Sure, we all love a beautiful floral arrangement, but one we can eat? Yes, please! A cookie bouquet makes for a memorable centerpiece or unique gift. This bright arrangement would be great for an Easter get-together or Mother's Day gift!

The light corn syrup in my royal icing recipe keeps these raised florals soft to the bite while still being able to handle and package with ease. Piping florals is all about the icing consistency. Add small amounts of icing sugar at a time to your piping consistency until it holds a stiff peak on the spatula (see page 17 for an example of stiff consistency icing). You want it thick enough to hold its form, but not so thick that it's hard to pipe. If you find that your petals start to melt into each other, the icing isn't thick enough. Always take the time to get your consistency right before decorating – trial and error is just a part of this!

COOKIE SHAPES:
- Two types of flowers - one with soft curves and the other with longer petals, a teardrop leaf and longer style leaf.

ICING COLORS & CONSISTENCIES:
- Piping and flood consistencies in light and dark green
- Piping consistency in yellow
- Thick consistency in pink and purple

DECORATIONS & COLORANTS:
- White nonpareil sprinkles
- Edible glitter

DECORATING TOOLS:
- 7 piping bags
- Clips
- Two petal shaped piping tips
- Scribe tool

SUPPLIES FOR CREATING THE BOUQUET:
- Cookie / lollipop sticks – a solid and sturdy stick, do not use paper straws for these
- Flower or other decorative pot
- Styrofoam ball
- Wooden skewer
- Scissors
- Hot glue gun and glue sticks
- Shred or tissue paper

See page 57 for how to bake cookie pops.

Flowers

Hold the piping bag at a side angle with the narrow end of the petal tip facing upward and the wide end towards the cookie.

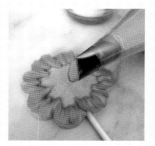  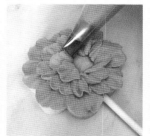 

PINK FLOWER:

1. Using a thick icing, pipe the first layer around the outer edge of the cookie in a ruffle sequence.

2. Pipe the second layer, slightly tipping the piping tip upward

3. Pipe a third and final layer of individual petals with the tip a little more upward.

4. Add some white nonpareil sprinkles to the center with edible glitter.

PURPLE FLOWER:

1. Using a thick icing, pipe the first layer of individual long, looped petals.

2. Pipe a second layer of alternating shorter loops, ending in the center of the cookie.

3. Use piping icing to pipe a larger yellow dot in the center, adding some white nonpareil sprinkles and edible glitter.

Leaves

1. Outline the two leaf styles with light and dark green piping icing.

2. Fill with coordinating light and dark green flood icing.

3. Once the icing has crusted over, use piping icings to pipe the veins of the leaves.

Assembly

Choose a pot size that will act as a sturdy base for your arrangement and plan how you want to arrange the bouquet. Keep the heavier florals more central and use the leaves as fillers to even out the overall look. If gifting, place a cellophane bag over top of the cookie and tie tightly with a ribbon around the stick.

The styrofoam must fit tightly inside the pot with no room to move around – you may need to cut it to size or secure with some smaller pieces around it. If using a circular styrofoam piece, cut the bottom to be flat. Add a bit of hot glue to secure to the bottom of the pot.

Continued on pg. 70

1. Use a wooden skewer to pre poke the holes in the styrofoam. The skewer should be slightly thinner than the cookie pop stick, just carving the way for it to be inserted without putting too much stress on the stick and cookie. Ensure you are leaving enough room between the cookies so that they don't rub together.

2. Insert the cookie pop into the hole and determine if the stick needs to be cut down depending on its placement. Make the sticks shorter in the front and taller in the back to showcase all of the cookies.

3. Once all cookie pops are in place, fill the base and any exposed Styrofoam with shred or tissue paper.

Easter: Watercolor Easter Eggs

I might be biased, but this is always my preferred method for Easter egg decorating and anyone can do them!

 The term watercolor for cookies is a little deceiving as it's actually alcohol that you want to use for it. Using this amount of water on dried icing can eat away at it while alcohol evaporates much quicker, leaving just the color. Don't worry – there's no residue or aftertaste and the cookie is still safe to eat for all ages. Don't forget to ice your cookies ahead of time so they are full dry when its time to paint!

COOKIE SHAPE:

- Egg

DECORATING TOOLS:

- Paint palette & paint brushes

- 1 piping bag

- Clips

ICING COLORS & CONSISTENCIES:

- Piping consistency in white

DECORATIONS & COLORANTS:

- Gel food colors

- Alcohol (vodka is best)

- Water for rinsing brushes

1. Add one drop of your selected gel food colors to the paint palette and mix with the alcohol until dissolved.

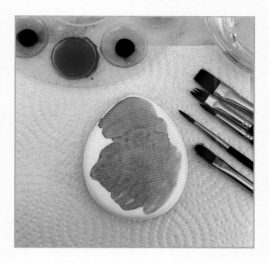

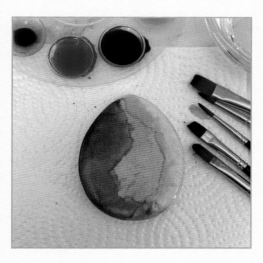

2. Use a paint brush to apply a base color that will blend well with the others. Rinse the brushes with water and pat dry when needed.

3. Paint on and slightly blend one or two more colors.

4. Keep blotting and layering these while incorporating other accent colors if desired. Let the colors naturally combine.

5. Once dry, use white piping consistency to create designs over top.

School Days

Whether you're upping your lunch box note game or gifting a hard working teacher, these cookies capture some of the hallmarks of school in a fun way!

Edible markers really bring this set to life with the lined note paper heart, chalkboard effect and simple details on the apple to tie it all together. Only use your markers on fully dry icing so that you don't puncture the surface or ruin the tips. If you don't have a white marker, you can use a bit of white food gel with a paint brush and water to create the chalkboard look, piping the words over top. Use a piping tip to cut the hole for the gummy worms into the dough before baking!

COOKIE SHAPES:

- Apple
- Heart
- Rectangle

DECORATING TOOLS:

- 8 piping bags
- Clips
- V shaped piping tip
- Scribe tool
- Icing scraper
- Flat paint brush

ICING COLORS & CONSISTENCIES:

- Piping and flood consistencies in red, white and brown
- Flood consistency in black
- Thick consistency in green

DECORATIONS & COLORANTS:

- Edible glitter
- Black, red, blue and white edible markers
- Gummy worms
- Water

1. Pipe a thick outline with brown piping icing.

2. Fill with black flood icing.

3. Once fully dry, draw lines over top of the black with a white edible marker and blend with a bit of water on a flat paint brush.

4. Once dry, write your message over top with white edible marker and pipe the apple and chalk with red, green and white piping icing.

1. Outline with white piping icing.

2. Flood with white flood icing.

3. Once fully dry, use the edge of an icing scraper or other food safe straight edged object to draw the lines with red and blue edible markers.

4. Use a black edible marker to write a message.

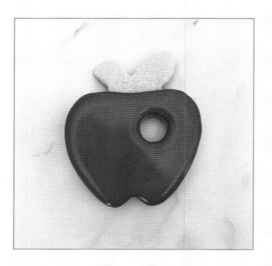

1. Outline the body of the apple with red piping icing.

2. Fill with red flood icing.

3. Ouline the stem with brown piping icing, adding zig squiggle lines inside to prevent cratering and fill with brown flood icing.

4. Use a v shaped piping tip to pipe the leaf with green thick icing. Apply pressure and release repeatedly to create the rippled effect. Add some edible glitter.

5. Once fully dry, add some definition with a black edible markers and insert the gummy worm through the hole.

Summer: Beach Days

Bring the brightness and fun of summer to life with your cookies! I'm usually from the camp of 'more is more', but the simplest of details can be all that's needed to bring a cookie set to life. Some basic piping and edible marker lines add definition while letting the colors really stand out!

Keep in mind when coloring your icing that both deep and bright colors will develop further after they are mixed. Even just an hour can make a big difference so plan to make these in advance when you can. Build your colors up when mixing so that you only use the amount of coloring needed and not oversaturate it which can cause colors to bleed together or potentially have an unpleasant taste.

COOKIE SHAPES:

- Bathing suit
- Palm leaf
- Popsicle
- Shorts
- Star fish

DECORATING TOOLS:

- 9 piping bags
- Clips
- Scribe tool
- Paint palette
- Paint brushes (flat, fan & dot)

ICING COLORS & CONSISTENCIES:

- Piping and flood consistencies in pink, turquoise, green and yellow
- Piping consistency in white

DECORATIONS & COLORANTS:

- Small and Large white sugar pearls
- Black edible marker

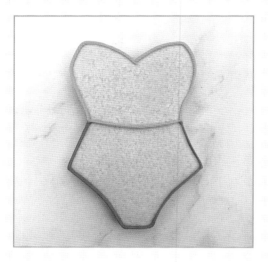

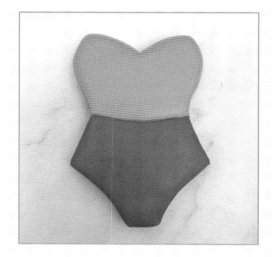

1. With piping consistencies, outline the top portion in pink and the bottom with green.

2. Fill the top with pink flood icing.

3. Once crusted over, fill the bottom with green flood icing.

4. Once fully dry, use white piping icing to pipe the detail lines and add the black edible marker details.

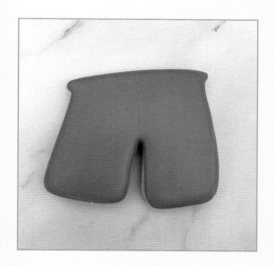

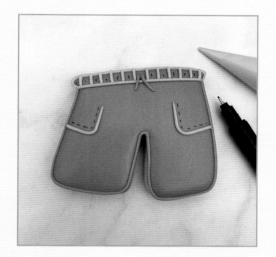

1. Outline with turquoise piping icing.

2. Fill with turquoise flood icing.

3. Once fully dry, use yellow piping icing to pipe the detail lines and add the black edible marker details.

Popsicle

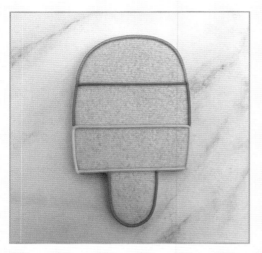

1. With piping icing, outline the stick with brown and three evenly spaced sections of the popsicle with pink, turquoise and yellow.

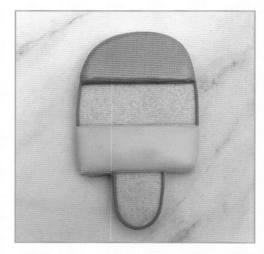

2. Fill the top and bottom portions of the popsicle with pink and yellow flood icing.

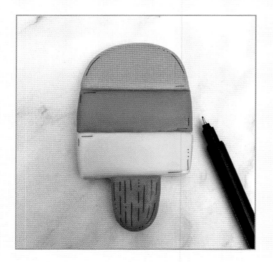

3. Once crusted over, fill the remaining sections with turquoise and brown flood icings.

4. Once fully dry, add the black edible marker details.

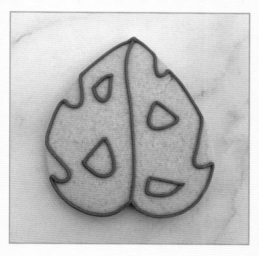

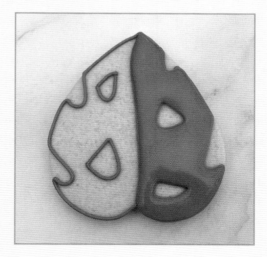

1. Use green piping icing to outline in two half sections, adding areas around the border and inside to form holes in the leaf.

2. Fill the first half of the leaf with green flood icing.

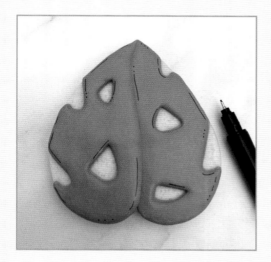

3. Once crusted over, fill the second half with green flood icing.

4. Once fully dry, add the black edible marker details.

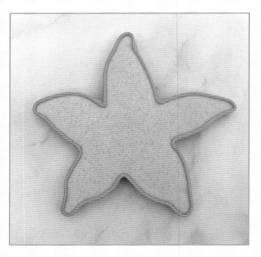

1. Outline with pink piping icing.

2. Fill with pink flood icing and place a large white sugar pearl in the center with smaller ones spaced outward.

3. Once fully dry, add the black edible marker details.

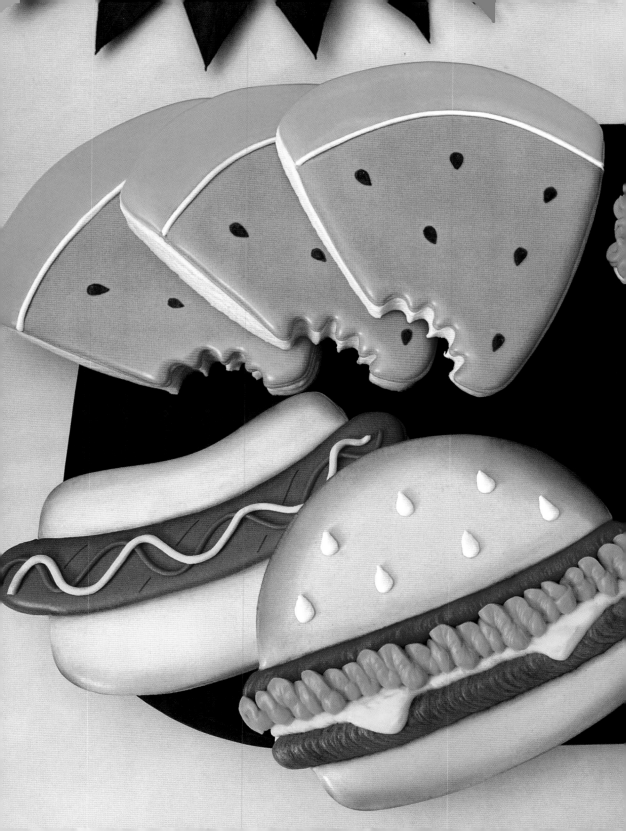

Summer BBQ

Summer is always a great time to gather outdoors with friends and family. Pass on bringing the salad next time and surprise everyone with dessert - no one will be complaining when they need to finish these veggies!

It's always safest to keep icing designs simple for warmer outdoor events. Royal icing doesn't melt but heat can cause elements like paints and airbrushing to smear or bleed together. A great way to add a little extra in these times is shading with dusts like shown on the hotdog and hamburger. A lot of the time you will see this done with an airbrush which adds color over top of icing, but dry dusting with a petal or luster dust actually colors the surface of the icing without potential for it to smear. You could use this effect on the watermelon and vegetables too to give the added dimension if you'd like!

Another little trick I want to share with you is how to pipe leaves and ruffles without a piping tip – yes, it's possible!

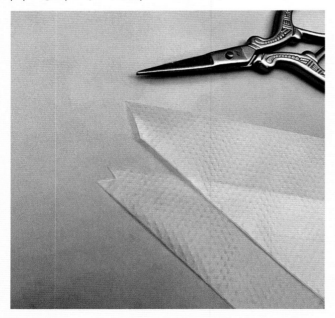

For both you want the tip of your bag completely flat with the seam to the side. For a leaf tip, cut an even v shape. For a petal tip to pipe ruffles or florals, cut a slant downward from the seam side over. The size that you cut will determine how large of a petal of leaf you get, so start on the small side if you aren't sure and you can make it bigger if needed.

COOKIE SHAPES:

- Broccoli
- Carrot
- Small circle
- Large circle
- Hamburger
- Hotdog
- Rectangle
- Watermelon

DECORATING TOOLS:

- 18 piping bags
- Clips
- V shaped leaf and petal piping tips (optional)
- Scribe tool
- Dust brush

ICING COLORS & CONSISTENCIES:

- Piping and flood consistencies in light brown, dark brown, light red, dark red, light green, dark green and orange
- Piping consistency in white & yellow
- Thick consistency in light and dark green

DECORATIONS & COLORANTS:

- Rainbow nonpareil sprinkles
- Brown petal dust
- Black edible marker

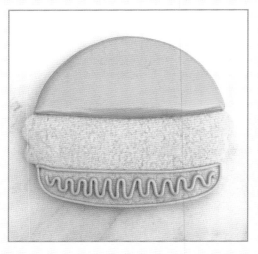

1. Outline the top and bottom buns with light brown piping icing, adding squiggle lines to the bottom to prevent cratering.

2. Fill both portions with light brown flood icing.

3. Once crusted over, use piping icings to add a dark brown patty with yellow cheese dripping over top, and red for a tomato under the top bun. Use a scribe to manipulate the icing and smooth where needed.

4. Pipe the lettuce as a ruffle using light green thick icing. You can cut the tip of the bag at a slant or use a petal piping tip.

5. Once fully dry, use a brown petal dust with a dust brush to apply shading around the buns – start very light and even, working the pigment up as you go.

6. Use white piping icing to pipe seeds on the top bun as teardrops, applying more pressure at first and releasing as you pull away.

Watermelon

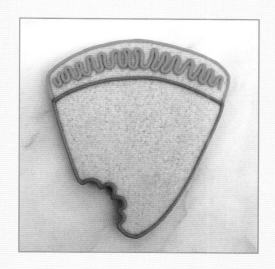

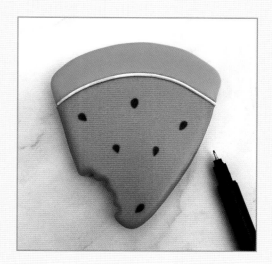

1. Use piping icings to outline the top and bottom portions with light green and light red.

2. Fill with corresponding flood icings.

3. Once crusted over, pipe a line in between the red and green sections with white piping icing.

4. Once fully dry, draw on the black edible marker seed details.

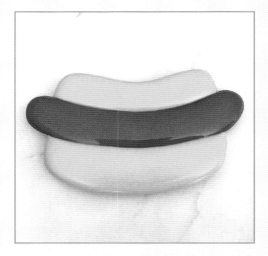

1. Use piping icings to outline the bun areas with light brown and the wiener with dark brown.

2. Fill with corresponding flood icings.

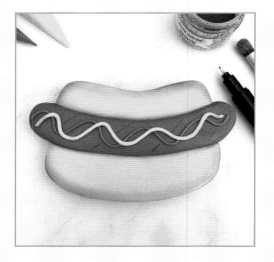

3. Once fully dry, use a brown petal dust with a dust brush to apply shading around the buns – start very light and even, working the pigment up as you go.

4. Draw slanted grill lines on the wiener using a black edible marker and then pipe two wavy lines with dark red and yellow piping icings to act as the ketchup and mustard.

Tomato

1. Outline with dark red piping icing.

2. Fill with dark red flood icing.

3. Once crusted over, pipe a leaf with dark green thick icing.

Broccoli

1. Outline the stem with dark green piping icing.

2. Fill with dark green flood icing.

3. Pipe small swirls with dark green thick icing, overlapping in different areas to create dimension.

Celery

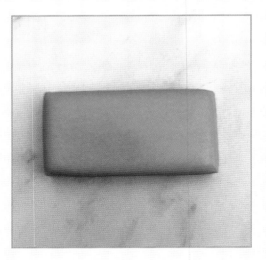

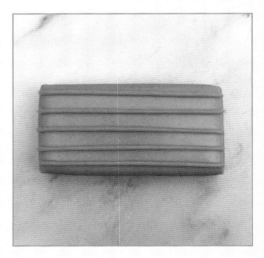

1. Outline with light green piping icing.

2. Fill with light green flood icing.

3. Once crusted over, use light green piping icing to pipe lines across.

Carrot

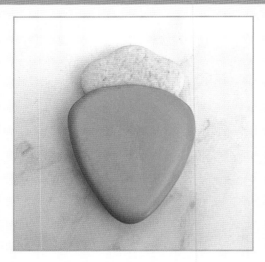

1. Outline the body with orange piping icing.

2. Fill with orange flood icing.

3. Pipe the leaves with dark green thick icing, moving the tip back and forth while alternating pressure. You can cut the tip of the bag as an inward v or use a v shaped piping tip.

1. Use dark brown piping icing to pipe a thick outline around the border. Use the end of your scribe tool or finger to gently create indents all the way around.

2. Fill the inside with white piping icing, swirling and smoothing out any areas needed with a scribe tool. Add rainbow nonpareils over top.

Thanksgiving & Fall

There's just something about that transition from Summer to Fall, adding on the layers with a warm drink and getting back to some routine. You'll be feeling thankful, grateful and blessed with these cozy Fall designs!

We'll be capturing some of those beautiful changing leaf colors with painting in this set. See page 26 for how to turn your dusts into beautiful paints!

COOKIE SHAPES:

- Coffee mug
- Two leaf styles
- Pumpkin
- Sunflower

DECORATING TOOLS:

- Piping bags
- Clips
- V shaped piping tip
- Scribe tool
- Paint palette
- Paint brushes (assorted flat and detail)

ICING COLORS & CONSISTENCIES:

- 10 piping and flood consistencies in pink, orange, brown and white
- Thick consistency in white and yellow

DECORATIONS & COLORANTS:

- Coordinating sprinkle mix
- Brown jimmy sprinkles
- Orange, yellow and burgundy petal dusts
- Gold luster dust
- Alcohol
- Edible glitter
- Edible marker

1. Outline the mug with pink piping icing, adding squiggles to the inside of the handle to prevent cratering.

2. Fill with pink flood icing.

3. Once crusted over, use thick white icing to pipe the whipped cream. Add sprinkles and edible glitter.

4. Once fully dry, use a black edible marker to write a message or saying. Start by writing the letters normally and then go back and thicken up different areas to give it more of a fun look.

1. Pipe a large circle to the middle using brown piping and top with brown jimmy sprinkles.

2. Using a thick yellow icing and a v shaped piping tip, pipe the first layer of petals to the existing petals of the cookie moving the tip back and forth while alternating pressure.

3. Pipe a second layer of smaller alternating petals.

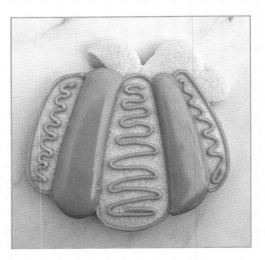 

1. Use orange piping icing to outline the pumpkin in sections, adding squiggles to each one to prevent cratering.

2. Fill alternating sections with orange flood icing.

3. Once crusted over, fill the remaining sections with orange flood icing.

4. Outline the stem with brown piping icing, adding a squiggle to prevent cratering.

5. Fill with brown flood icing.

6. Use brown piping icing to pipe the swirl coming off of the stem and add edible glitter.

1. Outline two different leaf styles with white piping icing.

2. Fill with white flood icing and let fully dry.

3. Prepare your paint and use a flat paint brush to paint a light and even base layer of edible paint to each with yellow for one and burgundy for the other.

4. Use detail brushes to blend in orange and burgundy lines to the yellow leaf, and yellow and orange to the burgundy leaf.

5. Use a flat brush to splatter gold paint over top and top with some edible glitter.

Halloween

Let's get spooky! Not that we really need even more sugar on Halloween, but I would gladly trade my candy for some of these cookies. From royal icing transfers to wet on wet, to painting with edible markers and bubble lettering, I'll be showing you some of my favorite tricks for these spooktacular treats!

Icing transfers like these spiders for the web cookie are a great way to add more defined details and have more flexibility with placement instead of piping them directly onto the cookie and realizing you would have rather had them somewhere else. It's important to use a piping consistency for these so that they hold their form and don't crater or melt

together. You can create transfers ahead of time by piping onto parchment paper. Once fully dry, carefully remove them and use a bit of icing to place onto the cookie. Icing transfers are especially great for large projects if you want to get some work done in advance!

For these spiders, I used a free template download and made the bodies and legs thicker so they wouldn't break. Use piping icing to pipe the legs first and then the body starting in the middle and outward. Use a scribe to smooth out and adjust where needed.

We'll focus a lot on avoiding craters in this set. A lot of decorators don't know what a crater is until it's too late, and while they can be very discouraging, you can avoid them with the right consistencies and technique. With bubble lettering specifically, you want your flood icing a bit thicker than normal and then place the completed lettering in front of a table fan for 10 minutes. This speeds up the drying process so that the icing has less of a chance to sink inward.

See page 22 for more on cratering.

See page 57 for how to bake cookie pops.

COOKIE SHAPES

- "Boo" lettering or other basic plaque
- Candy corn
- Small circle
- Fangs
- Spiderweb

DECORATING TOOLS

- 10 piping bags
- Clips
- Scribe tool
- Flat paintbrush

ICING COLORS & CONSISTENCIES

- Piping and flood consistencies in pink, orange, green, white, and black (ensure the black flood icing is thicker for piping letting)

DECORATIONS & COLORANTS

- Coordinating sprinkle mix
- Edible glitter
- Water
- Black and red edible markers

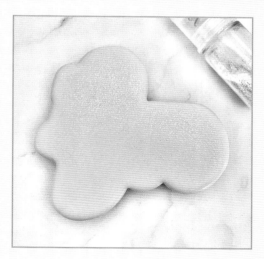

1. Outline the plaque with pink piping icing.

2. Fill with pink flood icing.

3. Once crusted over, apply some edible glitter.

4. Pipe the lettering so that the downstrokes can be filled, and the upstrokes remain just as a line. (it can help to have a projector for this, or practice first on some parchment paper so that you have a good idea of what you want it to look like). Add squiggles to the fill areas to prevent cratering.

5. Once crusted over, fill the down-strokes with a thick flood icing and smooth out with a scribe. Place in front of a table fan for 10 minutes.

1. Use a black edible marker to draw on the eyes and mouth with a guide line for the top of the bucket. Apply some edible glitter right away to the eyes and mouth.

2. Outline the outer border, eyes and mouth with orange piping icing.

3. Fill with orange flood icing.

4. Pipe a handle with black piping icing.

5. Apply white flood icing above the top of the bucket and place the sprinkles over top.

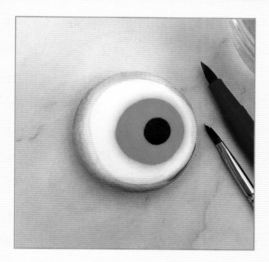 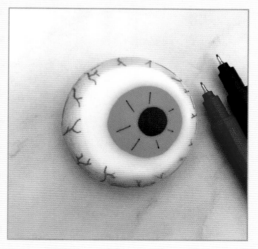

1. Outline with white piping icing.

2. Fill with white flood icing so that its slightly lower than usual, but even coverage. Immediately pipe an off-center green circle with flood icing and then a black circle to the center of the green with black flood icing.

3. Once fully dry, apply red edible marker around the border and blend with a damp flat paint brush.

4. Once dry, add the bloodshot lines with red edible marker and black detail lines to the green portion of the eye.

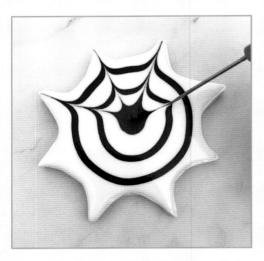

1. Outline the web with white piping icing.

2. Fill with white flood icing and immediately pipe two outer circles and a large dot in the middle with black flood icing.

3. Use a scribe tool to pull the icing from the middle black dot, outward to the tip of the web. Clean off the tip of your scribe before repeating around the web.

4. Once fully dry, use a bit of icing to carefully glue the spider transfers to the top of the cookie.

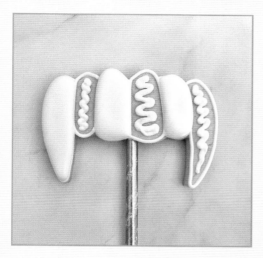

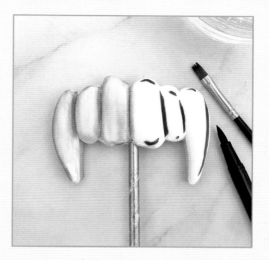

1. Use white piping icing to outline the teeth in sections, adding squiggles to each one to prevent cratering.

2. Fill alternating sections with white flood icing.

3. Once crusted over, fill the remaining sections with white flood icing.

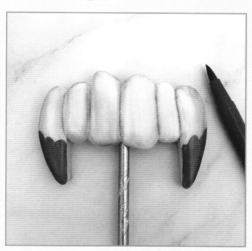

4. Once fully dry, apply black edible marker to the outer edges and creases of the teeth and use a damp flat paint brush to blend so that its darker around the edges and lighter on the inside of each tooth. Keep adding the edible marker ink and blending as needed.

5. Once fully dry, use a red edible marker to draw blood on each fang.

Christmas & Winter

If there's any holiday that's not complete without sugar cookies, it's Christmas! On the naughty list? Don't worry, we can fix that. There's just something extra cute about cookies that look like true cookies this time of year, and this faux gingerbread theme will have everyone feeling the holiday spirit.

Chocolate accents make a great addition to decorated cookies and can be made easily with silicone molds. Candy melts are a quick and convenient way to make them, where unlike pure chocolate that needs to be tempered, they can be heated in the microwave and used right away. Just like with fondant accents, you can make these in advance or have a variety on hand to speed up future projects!

COOKIE SHAPES:

- Gingerbread house
- Gingerbread person
- Heart
- Snowflake
- Tree

DECORATING TOOLS:

- Piping bags
- Clips
- Scribe tool
- Star shaped piping tip
- Dust brush
- Silicone bow mold
- Off set spatula

ICING COLORS & CONSISTENCIES:

- 7 piping and flood consistencies in pink white and brown
- Thick consistency in green

DECORATIONS & COLORANTS:

- Red candy melts
- Coordinating sprinkle mix
- Sugar Pearls
- Pearl luster dust
- Edible glitter
- Black edible marker

Candy melts come in a variety of colours or can be tinted with an oil based, fat soluble food colouring once melted (regular gel colours do not combine with oil based products like chocolate).You can also paint of dry dust depending of the look you would like!

STEPS FOR MAKING CHOCOLATE ACCENTS:

1. Place the melts in a microwave safe bowl and heat at 20 - 30 second increments, stirring in between. It usually takes 2 - 3 rounds of heating before the chocolate fully melts. Plan to melt the chocolate only when you are ready to use it.

2. Once fully melted, pour into a piping bag to pipe into the molds or use a spoon to scoop it in.

3. Use an off set spatula or any other flat food safe surface to level the top of the chocolate and place in the freezer for 5-10 minutes. Since chocolate solidifies quite fast, I like to keep it on a heating pad when not in use. You can also use a small melting pot or slightly warm stove top.

4. Carefully remove the chocolate accents once they have solidified and let the mold warm up before repeating.

Try to handle the accents as little as possible as the heat of your hand can mark them. Use a bit of icing to place onto the cookie when complete or store in an airtight container for later use.

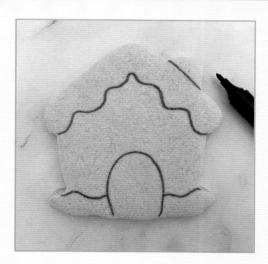

1. Draw piping guides for the top and bottom snow areas with an edible marker.

2. Outline the snow areas with white piping icing.

3. Fill with white flood icing and add sprinkles.

4. Once the snow areas have crusted over, apply edible glitter to them and then outline the sides of the house and chimney with brown piping icing and the door with pink piping icing. Add squiggles within the chimney and door to prevent cratering.

5. Fill the door chimney with brown flood icing and the door with pink flood icing.

6. Once the door has crusted, fill the remainder of the house with brown flood icing.

7. Once the base icing is crusted, pipe a beaded border around the sides and top of the door with pink piping icing. Apply pressure and release as you pull away forming a teardrop and slight overlap until complete. For the peppermints, pipe a dot of white piping icing and settle it out with a scribe tool. Use pink piping icing to pipe a swirl over top.

8. Once the base icing is fully dry, draw horizontal lines across the house and chimney, and a doorknob with a black edible marker. Use a bit of icing to glue the chocolate bow to the center.

1. Outline with brown piping icing.

2. Fill with brown flood icing and apply two sugar pearl buttons to the bodies.

3. Once fully dry, draw on the eyes, lashes, eyebrows, and mouths. Pipe a dot with white piping icing to the eyes.

4. Pipe squiggles as hair and across the hand and feet with white piping icing. Use a bit of icing to glue the chocolate bows to the head and neck.

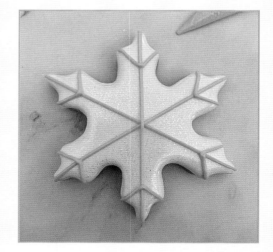

1. Outline with white piping icing.

2. Fill with white flood icing.

3. Once crusted over, apply edible glitter.

4. Use pink piping icing to pipe a design over top and place a sugar pearl in the center.

1. Pressure pipe the branches across the bottom layer with green thick icing in a tear drop motion, applying hard and slow pressure at first and lighter as you pull away.

2. Pipe each layer of branches, slightly overlapping the ones before it.

3. Apply sprinkles and edible glitter.

4. Pipe the tree stump with brown piping icing.

1. Outline with brown piping icing.

2. Fill with brown flood icing.

3. Once crusted over, pipe another off set, curvy outline with white piping icing.

4. Fill will with white flood icing and add sprinkles.

5. Once crusted over, apply some edible glitter.

Tutorials

Paint Your Own Cookies And Stenciling

Who says you can't play with your food? Interactive cookies are a hit for every occasion, especially for kids. Paint Your Own cookies (known as PYO for short) will allow you to share the fun of decorating with others by providing a delicious canvas with edible paint, and there are several ways to do them!

CREATE YOUR CANVAS

Provide a specific design or leave the options open. Be sure to take a picture, because these works of art don't typically last long!

BLANK COOKIE

The simplest option is, of course, a plain iced cookie that allows the artist to paint any image they want. With any style, you can incorporate the paint onto the same cookie or provide a second one to keep them separate.

MINIMAL DESIGN

Use specific shapes and define them with simple piped details that break up the space but allow for creative freedom.

STENCILING

Food safe stencils allow you to place a specific image onto the cookie to act as an outline for painting. Stenciling for PYO cookies must be done with royal icing as opposed to airbrushing or any other paint solution so that the outline doesn't smear when painted.

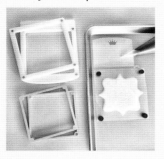

WHAT YOU NEED TO GET STARTED

- Stencil holder or magnets and a baking sheet
- Icing scraper
- Food safe stencils
- Iced and fully dry cookies
- Piping consistency icing

There are a variety of stencil holder options available for cookie decorating from a basic magnetic frame to more robust systems that allow you to adjust the height based on the thickness that you roll your cookies. You can even use magnets secured to a baking sheet and stack them to the height needed, securing them with another magnet over the top. Whichever option you use, ensure that the stencil lies flat over the top of the cookie without any gaps. A flat and smooth base layer of icing on the cookie is key for how the stencil sits over the top of it.

STEPS FOR STENCILING

1. Secure the stencil over the top of the cookie and apply piping consistency icing to a stencil scraper.

2. Scrape an even and generous first layer over the top of the stencil while keeping the holder or magnets in place.

3. Keep scraping the icing in the same direction to remove the excess icing while leaving the outline. Be careful not to push the icing underneath the stencil when scraping.

4. Lift the stencil upright and away from the cookie.

You can usually stencil 6–12 cookies before needing to rinse the stencil. Dry the stencil completely; any remaining water can cause smudging on the next cookies.

PREPARE THE PAINT

Next, you need to create a paint palette that the artist can activate with just a bit of water and a paintbrush. Airbrush color and edible markers are my go-to methods when making palettes because they provide the most pigment and dry fully. I will note that gel colors do work for a palette but can remain tacky, so they aren't ideal if you plan to package them.

EDIBLE INK PAPER PALETTE

Edible ink printed on food safe sheets of paper are a convenient option if you don't wish to make your own. They come in a wide range of colors and save a lot of time. Keep in mind that the colors appear darker on the paper than when painted.

EDIBLE MARKERS

Apply the ink from the marker directly onto the icing. Use a brush tip for the most coverage and apply 1–2 layers, being careful not to puncture the icing.

AIRBRUSHED COOKIE

Airbrush the color directly onto the icing, beginning with a light first layer and then another 1–2 layers. Leave a little bit of space between the colors so that they don't run together when painting. I recommend only using this method with a second cookie.

AIRBRUSHED ICING TRANSFERS

Airbrushed royal icing transfers can be made in advance and stored in an airtight container to be used whenever you need them.

STEPS FOR MAKING ICING PAINT TRANSFERS

1. Use a piping icing consistency that will hold its form but still settle smoothly with a scribe to pipe dots onto a piece of parchment paper. Keep in mind the size of cookie that they will be going on and how many colors will be needed.
2. Let the transfers dry in front of a fan for the first 10 minutes so that they don't develop any craters.
3. Once the transfers are about halfway to being fully dry (typically 3–4 hours), airbrush color onto them in 2–3 light layers.
4. Once the transfers are fully dry (typically 6–8 hours), remove them from the parchment paper and either store in an airtight container or glue onto a fully dry and iced cookie with some royal icing to adhere.

If packaging the airbrushed options within a sealed bag, apply a light layer of cornstarch over top of the colors once dry so that it absorbs any moisture that can form when cookies are sealed. Although they will look a bit duller in color at first, they will return to their original vibrancy while in the bag.

PAINTING THE COOKIE

Now for the fun part! You'll want to provide a food safe, soft-bristled brush with a paint-your-own set so that all you need is some water and a napkin or paper towel to bring it to life. These palettes can typically provide enough paint for 2–3 cookies, of course depending on the age and enthusiasm of the artist!

Airbrushing

It doesn't take long once you catch the cookie decorating bug to start thinking about the possibilities with airbrushing! From shading to background patterns and lettering, you can really take your designs to the next level. Just like when learning the core decorating techniques, airbrushing can be quite intimidating at first, but rest assured that once you get going with it that it will be hard to not want to airbrush all the things!

WHAT YOU NEED TO GET STARTED

- Airbrush system
- Airbrush cleaning solution
- Airbrush food colors
- Food safe stencils
- Paintbrush
- Scribe tool
- Spoon, pipette, and alcohol if using dusts
- Paper towel

AIRBRUSHING WITH READY-TO-USE LIQUID COLORS

Designed specifically for airbrushing, these colors are the easiest to use by simply adding to the well of the gun and spraying with a medium air flow.

Metallic colors are usually thicker and need a higher air flow to spray smoothly. You can also get upgraded airbrush guns specifically for metallics if you find that your regular gun has issues spraying them.

AIRBRUSHING WITH DUST FOOD COLORS

Any petal or luster dusts can be diluted with vodka to be used for airbrushing. Just like when painting with alcohol, it evaporates from the surface and leaves just the color on the icing and is safe for consumption. Use a small bowl to dilute the dust to a very thin consistency so that the liquid can run through the gun without clogging. Do so only when you are ready to airbrush because when the alcohol has time to evaporate, it will change the consistency. Use a pipette to transfer the liquid to the well of the gun and spray at the highest air flow setting. Always do a test spray on paper towel to ensure the liquid sprays smoothly, readjusting if needed. An upgraded gun can be beneficial if you do a lot of airbrushing with dusts as it allows for better flow of this type of coloring.

CARE AND MAINTENANCE

Airbrush systems are actually very easy to assemble. Proper care and maintenance are the most important factors to successful use.

Rinse your gun with water right after airbrushing by first rinsing out the well and then spraying water through the gun until it comes out clear. Run an airbrush specific cleaning solution through it after each airbrushing session so that any residual coloring doesn't clog the passageway. Metallics and dust solutions should never be left to sit for long periods, especially when using alcohol mixtures, as it can cause corrosion.

A deep clean should be done occasionally, depending on how much you use your airbrush, by taking the main pieces (nozzle and back end) of the gun apart and soaking them in the cleaning solution for a few hours or overnight. Let the pieces fully dry prior to reassembling.

Most problems that come about with the gun are a result of loose parts. If your gun isn't spraying properly, ensure that the nozzles, screws and interior pin are secure. Always refer to the manufacturer's guidelines and recommendations to ensure proper care and troubleshooting.

WHEN TO AIRBRUSH

Basic shading without any stencils can be applied as soon as the icing has crusted over. Airbrushing with a stencil and holder should only be done around the 8–10-hour mark so the icing can withstand pressure and the stencil doesn't stick to it. Airbrush color dries quickly and will remain without any smudging or bleeding if regular icing dry times and storage guidelines are followed (see pages 13 and 21).

BASIC TECHNIQUE

The first factor in successful airbrushing is a flat and smooth base layer of icing for the color to adhere to evenly. You only need to fill the well of the gun ½ to ¾ full at most so that you avoid any spills while airbrushing. As tempting as it is, you will never need to pull all the way back on that trigger. Always start light and build your color up in layers. Going in too strong causes the liquid to pool and form puddles—slow and steady really does win the race here! Give some space between the gun and the cookie so that the color sprays on light and evenly. Spray at a downward angle and never from the side to avoid under spray when using stencils.

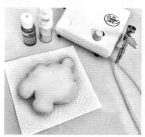

SHADING

If you're not a fan of mixing all the icing colors, you will love the ability to add color with airbrushing! From simple shading around the border to creating different multi-color effects, you can really add some depth and visual effects that otherwise can't be done with just icing.

BACKGROUNDS

From simple patterns to more intricate designs, using stencils for your backgrounds or even sole design of a cookie is a great way to bring the theme or overall feel of a set to life.

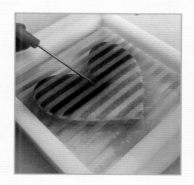

AIRBRUSHING WITH STENCILS

1. Secure the stencil over top of the cookie so that it lies flat. Look for any areas that that may pop up so that you can use a scribe to hold them down if needed.

2. Spray on a light and even layer of color, pulling the lever of the gun back gently while following the natural design of the stencil. Position the gun above as vertical as possible so that the color doesn't spray under the stencil.

3. Apply a second layer of color following the same steps as the first. Keep the gun moving; don't airbrush in one area for too long to avoid pooling. You should only need 2–3 total layers of color to achieve a solid coat.

4. Remove the stencil upward and away from the cookie while being careful not to smudge the lines. Repeat the process, rinsing the stencil and patting dry when needed.

5. Use a slightly damp paintbrush for any minor touch-ups. Brush very lightly, and clean off the brush after each stroke so that it doesn't smear the color.

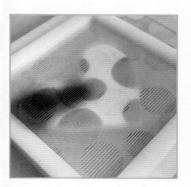

LAYERED STENCILS

Once you are comfortable with single designs, you can start layering! Layered stencil sets come with 2–4 stencils, depending on the design. Each layer will have cut outs and imprints of the others so that you can line them up easily. You'll want to plan the colors to blend well if they overlap and follow the same core steps for airbrushing, letting each layer dry for about a minute in between.

LETTERING

Not all of us are blessed with the ability to pipe perfect lettering. Luckily, stencils can take care of that for you! Because lettering and other more intricate stencil designs can have a lot of curves and various widths throughout, it can be more challenging to achieve crisp lines. When the risk of under or overspray is higher despite technique, consider using a silk screen, which goes directly over top of stencil and facilitates the color applying neatly within the cut-outs. You will need to use more color to get through the screen than without, but you don't need to worry as much about technique since the screen does the harder work for you!

 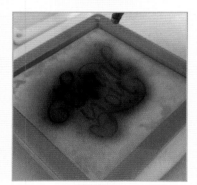 

STEPS FOR AIRBRUSHING WITH A SILK SCREEN

1. Place the silk screen directly above the stencil.

2. Spray on 2–3 layers of color, pulling the lever of the gun back gently while following the natural design of the stencil. Ensure that the color saturates all the way through.

3. Remove the stencil and screen upward and away from the cookie while being careful not to smudge the lines. Repeat the process, rinsing both the stencil and screen when needed and pat dry.

AIRBRUSHED ACCENTS

Airbrushing is a great way to add color to icing transfers, fondant accents, and more. You can also use the colors for painting details!

Packaging Decorated Cookies

Now that you have put all that effort into creating beautiful cookies, you want to showcase them in the best way, too! When gifting or selling, you can't always control exactly how they'll be handled, so ensure they are packaged with care before they leave you.

HEAT SEALING AND BAGS

One of the best things you can do is heat seal your cookies, which will extend their shelf life up to 3–4 weeks. This is very easy to do. Remember that the icing must be fully dry before bagging!

Cellophane bags work the best, and it's good to have a few sizes on hand. The most common sizes for decorated cookies are 3x5", 3x8", 4x6" and 5x7". An impulse heat sealer is then used to close off the top of the bag. Simply place the cookie in the bag and position the top under the sealer, closing the lever over the top with just a bit of space above the end of the cookie for a few seconds or until the light on the side turns off. Cellophane bags only need a medium heat setting to seal. You can adjust the heat setting to where you find it works the best. Trim the top of your bag, or leave it longer and tie some ribbon around it just above the seal.

If you don't have a heat sealer, use ribbon to tie the top of the bags as airtight as possible and they will remain fresh for a few days. For cookie pops, place the bag over the top and tie tightly with ribbon around the stick. There's no option for heat sealing these, so plan to make them as close to the occasion as possible.

BOXES

Window boxes provide a secure space while still showcasing designs. They come in a variety of sizes to accommodate anything from 2 cookies to a few dozen. Use crinkle paper on the bottom to cushion the cookies, if needed, so that they fit securely and don't move around.

SMALL CLEAR BOXES

These are great for displaying individual cookies or PYO sets. You can add colored cardstock to the back or even special occasion cards or gift cards. The most common sizes for cookies range from 4–6 inches.

PERSONALIZATION

This is where it gets fun if you want to take it there! There's no shortage of options when it comes to ribbons and bows to give your packaging a custom look. You can add custom tags, logos, and ingredient lists if needed.

SHIPPING COOKIES

There's no doubt that you'll have friends, family, or customers requesting that you send them your cookies!

You'll need two boxes. The first one will be used to place individually wrapped or heat-sealed cookies upright inside with bubble wrap between them. Ensure the box fits them well and that any extra room is filled with the bubble wrap as well. Tape this box closed and then set it inside of a slightly larger box, filling the gaps between them with bubble wrap, packing peanuts, or anything else that will cushion any possible impact.

Resources

Be sure to check out our online shop, Cookie Couture, for all your tool and supply needs! We carry a great selection of cookie cutters and I love to support other small shops too! Here is a list of the makers for all of the cutters used in this book.

BIRTHDAY
Cupcake: Ann Clark
Candle, present, and balloon: Kaleidacuts
Plaque: Killer Zebras

WEDDING
All cutters: The Cookiery

BABY
Girl and boy outfits and bib: Ann Clark
Bottle, rattle, and dream
catcher: The Cookiery

VALENTINE'S
Conversation Heart: Killer Zebras
Lips and Hershey's kiss: The Cookiery
Strawberry: The Cookie Countess
Ice Cream Cone: Ann Clark

ST PATRICK'S
Shamrock: Ann Clark

COOKIE BOUQUET
Flowers and teardrop leaf: Ann Clark
Long leaf: The Cookiery

EASTER EGGS
Egg: Ann Clark

SCHOOL
Apple and Rectangle: Ann Clark
Heart: Sweet Sugarbelle

BEACH DAYS
Bathing suit and swim shorts: Kaleidacuts
Starfish, palm leaf, and popsicle: Ann Clark

BBQ
Burger: Killer Zebras
Hotdog: Ann Clark
Vegetable set and watermelon: The Sugar Shoppe

THANKSGIVING
Coffee mug, sunflower, and leaves: Ann Clark
Pumpkin: Killer Zebras

HALLOWEEN
Boo plaque: Kaleidacuts
Candycorn / pumpkin: Sweet Sugarbelle
Vampire teeth: Wilton
Small circle and spiderweb: Ann Clark

CHRISTMAS
Heart: Sweet Sugarbelle
Gingerbread house and people: The Cookiery
Tree and snowflake: Ann Clark

PAINT YOUR OWN
All Cutters: Ann Clark

AIRBRUSHING
All cutters: Killer Zebras

About the Author

Corianne Froese is the Founder of Cookie Couture, an online baking supply boutique where you'll find everything you need to create one-of-a-kind cookies and other treats. Having started out with no prior baking experience, Corianne learned everything through trial and error, soon growing her hobby into an award-winning home bakery, teaching sold-out workshops, and inspiring thousands with her online decorating videos. Known for her use of vibrant colors and bold but achievable designs, she has helped many grow their own passion and style of cookie decorating. In sharing her experiences, work, and life online, she's grown a dedicated following as a relatable and trusted expert in her field.

Website: www.coriannescustomcookies.com

Instagram: @_cookie_couture

Facebook: @shopcookiecouture